GW00787231

THE DARKER SIDE OF LOVE

Paper Swans Press

First published in Great Britain in 2015
by Paper Swans Press

ISBN 978-0-9931756-0-2

Printed in Great Britain by Jasprint

paperswans.co.uk
editor@paperswans.co.uk

CONTENTS

INTRODUCTION

Paper Swans Press is an independent publisher, dedicated to supporting the work of new and emerging writers, as well as celebrating the success of more established writers and poets. Started in 2014, we publish quarterly iPamphlet of poetry and flash fiction, which are downloadable from our website, and 'The Darker Side of Love' is our first printed anthology.

Through our website and now, as a small press, we strive to publish high quality writing and showcase some of the amazing talent that is emerging. Although based in the UK, we welcome submissions from writers all over the world - further details can be found on our website, paperswans.co.uk.

'The Darker Side of Love' was conceived as a reaction to the rose-tinted picture of love that is often portrayed through the media and rammed down our throats each January, as the frenzied build-up to Valentine's Day takes hold. As many of us know, romance can be brief and what is often found in relationships not sugar-coated, but bitter, dark and destructive. We wanted to give a collective voice to the rejected, the damaged and the vengeful. It proved to be a popular topic and so, this anthology was born.

Sarah, Stephanie & Ellie.

THE DARKER SIDE
OF LOVE

CKNOWLEDGEMENTS

:t' was made into a poem film by Abigail Norris and features in Maggie's live literature performance
mes of Avoidance'.

; Evening Falls' has been published in Orbis poetry magazine.

ie Day She Dropped' was first published online on Poetry School's Campus Blog in September, 2014.

ie Killing' was first published on the Ink, Sweat and Tears website in September 2014.

LEWIS BUXTON

THE MUSEUM OF BROKEN RELATIONSHIPS

Send us your ticket stubs,
the ones you keep piled in that drawer.
Send the poems written on the corner of napkins in pubs,

the t-shirts she/he left at your house,
send the photographs. We will respect them
as we would respect our own broken hearts.

Send the curl of hair left on the lino
of your bathroom floor; the scrunchy,
soggy in the shelf suctioned onto the shower door.

Bubble wrap the pictures;
the bracelets; the earrings; the payslips;
we'll display them, nameless on podiums three feet high

next to manikins wearing
the headdress and Stetson from Halloween
costumes that on reflection were definitely racist.

We know, it's like posting away a part of yourself
but we promise you'll feel better if you send them to us.
We will put them on show in cases with glass panelling,

people will be charged for the pleasure of seeing your suffering.
They'll see the tension, how your friends became the string
between two tin cans that you spoke to each other down.

So send us your lives, the texts, the emails, the letters.
Send us your bleeding hearts, the bloodier the better.
Send us the final straw, the last chance, send us the end of your tether.

FOR SALE

Come, see the hearts
laid out in lines, ready

to be parcelled up, carried
carefully away. Play

among the fresh stock,
give no thought to right

or wrong, muscle in on secret
songs. Find the fine line of love

if you dare but take care
not to linger. Some songs

can't be forgotten, some beats
are just too strong.

LYDIA POPOWICH

MY FIRST LOBSTER

My lover brought me a lobster
fresh from the Pentland Firth.
My lover wove the creel, steered the boat,
laid the trap, hauled the rope,
boiled the catch.

The lobster was beautiful,
pink naked in newspaper.
My lover said, the best is in the tail.
I tore the claws and knuckles, butter sticky,
sucking, licking, probing, splitting,
searching soft white meat.

Afterwards,
shell broken, belly filled with seawater
I dreamed of the ocean floor
and my lover waiting.

REFRESHMENT

Sheathed in darkness, I brew at the bar,
getting stronger every minute. You clasp
your hand around my waist, bring me
to your lips and taste me.

I am not sweet;
milky words do not sooth my bitterness.
You push me aside and I grow cold;
I am not your cup of tea.

THE DRESS

The white dress stained with red wine, now destined for the tip,
was the white dress worn to a wedding by the woman who,
preferring the magic of dogs, didn't feel the urge to marry.

The incident with the red wine didn't occur at the wedding
of the friend of the woman who preferred dogs, but when
the woman wore the white dress one winter to the wake of

an old soak in the drizzle-eyed County of Cork. It was the fate of
the white dress stained with red wine to outlive the woman
who, preferring the magic of dogs, & who wasn't destined

for wifehood, fell one day from a sleigh being pulled by
a fleet of sleet-eyed huskies, into the conjured snow of
the Finnmark Tundra in the friskiest year of her singular life.

WORTH

A dog pissing on a lamppost
you marked me, as yours, to love
like a tall tulip; ruined
by the first kiss
of heavy rain.

ACT

I wasn't cut out to be a Joan of Arc.
It was a mistake. My ears became immune

to the same old tune. I've made my choice,
shut the door, shunned the glory.

I've morphed you, my love, into a wolf
in kid's clothing, a baby-faced liar.

And though your howls infiltrate my dreams,
I will not stray from the path.

I'll recover my smile, reclaim my laugh.
Yes, I'm okay, since you inquire. I'm okay. Okay?

Except – except. Look here.
What's this? Is this my soul? Is it on fire?

LYDIA POPOWICH

THE DAY SHE DROPPED

the trifle, it exploded on the blue floor pain
-ting cryptic signs churned in chaos.
Raspberries, cream, vanilla custard, glace cherries, perfect
sponge, (home-made of course) secrets
hinted by hundreds and thousands
no-one would ever understand. The cold
glister of broken crystal, the old bowl her ex
brought back from Paris at his own risk.
She wanted to laugh until she saw
his face at the head of the table, the half
-empty bottle of Smirnoff, his plate strewn with left-over
Christmas, the scrunched up paper napkin, handy for blood
spilt when she tried to pick up the pieces.

ELISABETH SENNITT CLOUGH

SILVERFISH

The South Limburg house I lived in,
its basement pillowed on three sides
by moist Dutch earth, was ripe
for lepisma saccharina, the sweet
scrim of book glue seduced them,
until they flattened themselves between
white spaces and black words,
their inky mouths crumpling pages
of classics and not the good soil
my landlord said they were a sign of.

Paper faces in pictures were thinned out,
creped at the edges. From time to time
they suffocated from their small fry vandalism,
as I found guilty bodies framed against the glass
in places. I half-filled the shot glasses he'd left,
arranging sugar solutions as traps –
Tokyo, with its brown sticky tape
blacking out the Ginza District, then Jakarta
with a sellotape strip for climbing up
and over the Monas. Headfirst, they thrashed
their tails into a sweet descent, my tiny mermaids,

just as I had done decades earlier
as I fell from a plinth of high kerb, a line
of small glasses in the bar behind me, spent
in one sudden blast, as cartridge shells,
after he'd said goodbye, left me to walk out
into a wet night, where blues, greens and golds
lured me down into the fill of fluid,
my scales shattering on the concrete, like glass.

GILL McEVOY

OLD WOUNDS

'Because of your love', you wrote me once,
quoting from a poem I didn't know,
'there is gold in the depths of my dreams'.
Where are those dreams now? By chance,

polished by all the years I clutched it tight,
time left me one small thing, a stone,
of all those simple gifts you brought:
the beetle's wing that glowed with burnished light,

a leaf, a fragile bird-bone, natural things that I
delighted in. Time, they say, will heal. I say no:
Wounds and bruises deepen. In my sleep
they burrow in and sharply let me know

that love lasts beyond the point
at which, you think, you'd let it go.

KAY BUCKLEY

YOUR TRAINERS

I wonder if you still collect Adidas trainers,
and are they still kept pristine in their boxes
like small coffins of preserved joy;
and do you still leave that worn pair by the door,
that every day or every way not-noticed-pair
for someone, someone not me, to trip over?

JANUARY 31ST

I'm in that last year. The final one before you can throw all your tax stuff out; every taxi receipt, invoice sheet, what you spent since 2006. And I'm in that bracket now. Next year, you'll slip outside copyright like a hundred year old book and anyone can broadcast you then, play or perform, use a hologram version of you in an ad as everyone's dead to protest. The deadline creeps like a digital electricity meter. I watch each un-understandable increment, on the comfortable side of the decimal point. Letters aside, were you MINE? Was I right to log you next to Terry, Jenny and Jim? Or are you S's, the way Kim's been god's since millennium? Because there's no point paying tax twice on something. We should really figure this out.

THE SHIRT

After you'd gone
        I had to keep busy.
The kitchen shone as never before,
there was no ring around the bath,
the books on the shelf were in order,
every tin and every packet in the cupboard
was within date. And then,
for the first time since 1998,
I reached the bottom of the ironing basket
where your favourite shirt -
the one that was hard to iron -
lay crumpled
        as you had

ELLIE DANAK

THE KILLING

I've been staring
at the mobile phone
for too long. Now
it turns cold like a stone.
The screen mirrors
the bruised moon, litters
the sky with your name.
On the bedroom wall
your photo left
a raw square.

EMMA LEE

AS EVENING FALLS

I track the indentation
in your pillow
aware of sloughed cells
I can't see,
and can almost
feel the warmth
left by your skin,
a faint lingering
like a trace of scent.
I lean towards
the curve of your spine,
my hand slides down
each imagined vertebra,
my body curling
round where it knows
you would lie
if you weren't
in too much pain
for my touch.
If you were here
and not
where it smells of disinfectant
and always
seems to be twilight.

TRIOLET FOR M

last night he looked at me with eyes
as blue as Ireland is green
the touch of unexpected silk—surprise
last night he looked at me with eyes
the colour of those hot and windless August skies
that pulse with summer lightning: seen/unseen
last night he looked at me with eyes
as blue as Ireland is green

ELLIE DANAK

I AM NOT A MERMAID

One night, just before you turned your back
on my scorching lips, you complained about the reek

of fish in the house, hollow crab shells stuck
between your toes, sand on floors, popping

bladderwrack. I told you about my dream.
How trapped inside a stranded whale

carcass on a beach I heard primal screams
escape its ribcage. You loved the forbidden flesh

the pleasure of killing such a beast.
I filed down the edges of my scales, ironed my fin

into a cleaved heart. Your hands cupped
over my fused thighs; the farther away I drifted

the tighter the knot. My last memory of you:
behind a toughened glass you sketched

a monster, a woman, a hollow husk.

ABOUT THE POETS

STEPHANIE ARSOSKA
Stephanie has had work published by The Emma Press, Prole, Iron Press, Mother's Milk Books Magma, Ink, Sweat & Tears and Nutshells & Nuggets. She was a finalist in the Stanza digital slam and was featured on the IndieFeed Spoken Word podcast. She blogs at stephaniearsoska.co.uk where she also runs a Virtual Open Mic Night.

KAY BUCKLEY
Kay Buckley lives in Barnsley and writes poetry in between working full time for Children and Young People's Services. In 2013 she received funding for a Mentoring Programme run by Writing Yorkshire. Her poem 'Huskar' was overall winner of the 2014 York Mix Poetry Competition. Her poems have been published in magazines including Butcher's Dog and Brittle Star. You can find her on Twitter: @KayLBuckley

LEWIS BUXTON
Lewis Buxton is a North London based writer, he has been commissioned by companies like Tullamore D.E.W, Bittersuites and Body Gossip U.K. In 2014 he wrote for Moving Point Productions, creating the story and poems for 'The Improvised History of the World'. He graduated from University of East Anglia in 2014 and has run performance poetry and live literature events in both Norwich and London since 2012. In 2013 he founded Burn After Reading Presents, a poetry event in East London that has hosted some of the best poets working in the UK. He has been published online and in print by Kumquat Poetry, Word Bohemia and AYP Publishing. His new two person poetry show is in production hoping to tour in 2015

ELLIE DANAK
Ellie Danak is an Edinburgh-based poet with a background in researching modern Swedish crime novels. Her work has been published by The Emma Press, Plum White Press and it appeared on the Ink, Sweat and Tears, Black & BLUE and Poetry School Campus websites. She occasionally tweets here: @PoetryandPandas

EMMA LEE
Emma Lee has published 'Mimicking a Snowdrop' (Thynks Press), 'Yellow Torchlight and the Blues' (Original Plus) and 'Ghosts in the Desert' is forthcoming from Indigo Dreams Publishing in 2015. She blogs at emmalee1.wordpress.com and is a blogger-reviewer for Simon and Schuster. She also reviews for The Journal, London Grip and Sabotage Review magazines.

AMY MACKELDEN
Amy Mackelden lives in Newcastle upon Tyne. She won a Northern Promise Award from New Writing North in 2011 and co-founded northern poetry magazine Butcher's Dog. She co-edits Feminist Trash TV blog Clarissa Explains Fuck All, and is working on her first collection.

GILL McEVOY
Publications: 'The Plucking Shed', Cinnamon Press 2010; 'Rise' Cinnamon Press 2013; 'The First Telling' Happenstance Press, 2014. Gill lives in Chester where she runs several regular poetry events, plus occasional ones. Owns a perfectly golden, loopy Lurcher. She is a Hawthornden Fellow.

SARAH MILES
Sarah writes poetry and flash fiction and has been published by Forward Poetry, Word Bohemia and had a poem featured in the Canterbury Wise Words Literary Festival, 2014. She won a national writing competition with a piece of flash fiction and writes book reviews for an educational magazine. She is a teacher and lives in Sussex. Twitter: @_sarahmiles_

LYDIA POPOWICH
Lydia Popowich studied creative arts in Newcastle during the nineties. She worked for many years as a Community Artist involved in the Disability Arts Movement. She now lives with a black and white Orcadian cat called Hope, near the sea in the Far North of Scotland. She continues to write and make art. Her poems have appeared in Obsessed with Pipework, Northwords, Dream Catcher, The Dalesman and local anthologies.

MAGGIE SAWKINS
Maggie Sawkins won the 2013 Ted Hughes Award for New Work in Poetry for her live literature production 'Zones of Avoidance.' She lives in Southsea where she works with people in recovery from addictions. Her two collections are 'Charcot's Pet' (Flarestack) and 'The Zig Zag Woman' (Two Ravens Press). http://zonesofavoidance.wordpress.com

ELISABETH SENNITT CLOUGH
Elisabeth Sennitt Clough is a mother of three, wife and poet – not necessarily in that order. She has just returned to the UK after spending nearly a decade living and working overseas. She has been published in various UK magazines and anthologies.

MADELAINE SMITH
Madelaine Smith started writing poetry at about the age of seven but allowed herself to be distracted by life and the writing of teen novels (which remain unpublished). A series of unrelated events set Madelaine writing poetry again in 2010 and she has since had work published in several local anthologies, and in a number of e-publications. Madelaine has worked in bookselling, publishing, theatre, museums and was for a short time editor of The New Writer magazine.

NIA SOLOMON
Nia Solomon is a poet from Devon, currently working on the project Pictures for Poetry Proceeds for People, a collection of feminist poetry aimed at engaging non-poetry readers and non-feminists! This is her first published poem.

LAWRENCE WILSON
Lawrence grew up near Chicago, Illinois. He holds a BFA degree (hons) in drama, an MA in education and an MFA in interdisciplinary art. In a turnabout of his great-grandparents trans-Atlantic emigration in the 1890s, he moved to the UK in 2005, where he is currently head of English and drama at one of the oldest prep schools in England. He sings and acts professionally and has exhibited his pottery, sculpture, collages, installations and artist's books throughout the USA and Europe and online. His poetry, short fiction and essays have appeared in Agenda, Albedo One, Poet's Cove, Art and Academe, Prairie Light Review, The Art of Monhegan Island, on Salon.com, Monhegan.com and in other journals and anthologies.